My Own Special Way

Mithaa alKhayyat

Translation by Fatima Sharafeddini

Retold by Vivian French

Illustrated by Maya Fidawi

Orion
Children's Books

First published in the United Arab Emirates in 2010
by Kalimat Publishing & Distribution
This translated edition first published in Great Britain in 2012
by Orion Children's Books
a division of the Orion Publishing Group Ltd
Orion House
5 Upper St Martin's Lane
London WC2H 9EA
An Hachette UK Company

1 3 5 7 9 10 8 6 4 2

The Orion Publishing Group's policy is to use papers that are natural,
renewable and recyclable products and made from wood grown in sustainable
forests. The logging and manufacturing processes are expected to conform
to the environmental regulations of the country of origin.

A catalogue record for this book is available from the British Library.

ISBN 978 1 4440 0320 8

Printed and bound in China

www.orionbooks.co.uk

Contents

One

Hamda had four big sisters, and their names were Hind, Fatima, Jamila and Alya.

When Hamda asked if Hind would
play tea parties, Hind shook her head.

"I'm going to see my friend Sonya,"
she said. "We're going to
make necklaces."

"That sounds fun!" said Hamda.
"Can I make necklaces too?"

"No," said Hind. "You're too little.
Why don't you play tea parties with
your dolls?"

Hamda went to find Fatima.
Fatima was getting ready to go
shopping with Jamila. Hamda jumped
up and down in excitement.

"I love shopping! Are you going now this minute? Can I come with you?" she asked.

"No," said Fatima as she put on her coat.

Jamila gave Hamda a hug. "You're too little," she said. "Go and find Alya."

Alya was busy in the kitchen.

"What are you doing?" Hamda asked.

"My friend Salma is coming today,"
Alya said. "We're going to make cakes."

Hamda clapped her hands.
"Can I make cakes too?"

"No," said Alya. "You're too little."
She gave Hamda a kiss. "Go and play
with your toys."

Hamda felt cross, and she felt lonely, and she felt left out. She stomped into the sitting room where Mama was reading, and frowned.

"Dear me," said Mama. "You don't look very happy. What's the matter?"

"All my sisters are big," Hamda said.
"They say I'm too little to play with
them. When am I going to be big?"

Mama laughed. "Your sisters were
little once, just like you. Look!" She
pointed to the photos on the wall.

"Oh," said Hamda, and she went
to look at the photos.

Mama was right.

Hamda looked and looked, and she thought and thought.

At last she had an idea ... an idea all of her very own.

Two

That evening they all sat down for dinner. Hamda watched her sisters, and smiled a little secret smile.

"You're very quiet tonight, Hamda,"
Hind said. "What's wrong?"

Hamda shook her head. She didn't say
anything.

Jamila put down her fork.
"Is it a game?"

Hamda shook her head, and she smiled.

"Tell us!" said Alya. "Please tell us why you're smiling!"

"I'm not going to be little any more!"
Hamda said. "I know what makes you
big girls. You wear the veil when you
go out, and I'm going to wear it too!"

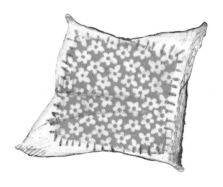

Hind, Fatima, Jamila and Alya
stared at their little sister.

"What is it?" Hamda asked.
She folded her arms. "I've made up
my mind. I want to wear the veil."

Hind gave Hamda a kiss. Fatima and Jamila gave her a hug. Alya kissed her too, and so did Mama.

"Why are you all kissing and hugging me?" asked Hamda.

"Because this is a special day,"
said Mama. "You're a big girl now –
and you found out how to do it
all by yourself!"

Three

Hind took Hamda's hand.
"Come on," she said. "Let's see what
we can find!"

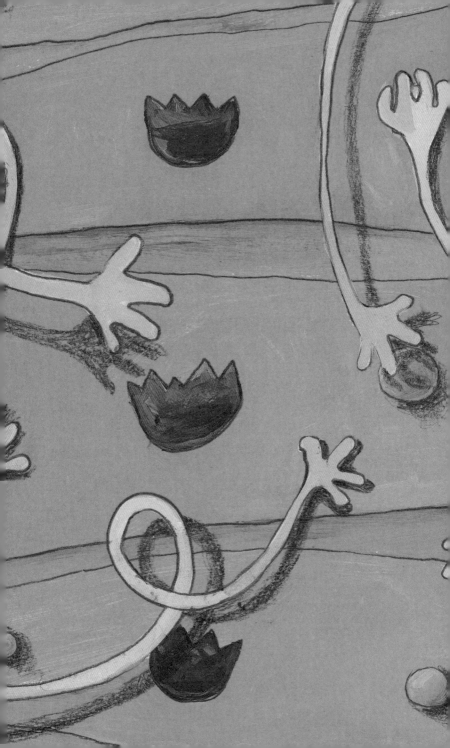

They pulled out one
drawer after another ...
and there were so many
headscarves!

"I've got lots too," said
Fatima, and she fetched
a big basket.

"And me," said Jamila,
and she emptied a box
all over the floor.

"Choose one of mine," said Alya.

She opened a cupboard and pulled out handfuls of scarves.

Hamda picked up the scarves, and threw them in the air.

Then Hamda stopped. She looked
worried. "I want to wear the veil," she
said. "But I don't know what to do."

"First," said Hind, "you must
choose a scarf."

Hamda picked up one scarf, and then another. At last she chose a black one covered in little red roses. "This is the nicest," she said.

"It suits you," said Hind. "Now, watch carefully. I put on a head cover to keep my hair tidy."

"OK," Hamda said. She chose a blue head cover, and slid it over her head.

Hind nodded. "Then I take a scarf, and place it over my head. Easy!"

Hamda picked up the black scarf with red roses, and put it on. "Look at me!" she said.

She ran out of the bedroom. Before she was halfway across the landing the scarf fell off. Hamda put it back on, and took two more steps. The scarf fell off for the second time.

"Oh no!" said Hamda. She tried a third time. The scarf fell off **again.**

Hamda went back to tell her sisters.

"Don't worry," said Fatima. "I know a better way."

Fatima draped a scarf over her head.
Then she tied the ends at the back of
her neck. "See? It doesn't move! I can do
anything and it doesn't ever fall off."

"Wow!" Hamda did a little twirl. "I'll wear it like that!"

"Shall I tie it for you?" Fatima asked.

"No! I want to do it on my own," Hamda said. She managed to tie a knot – but she tied it too tightly.

"Ooof! Ooof! Oof!"
she shouted.

"I can't breathe!"

She pulled the scarf off and dropped it on the floor. She was trying hard not to cry. "I'm **never** going to get it right."

Four

"Cheer up, little sister," Jamila said.
"Try wearing the veil the way I do.
It's very pretty. All my friends copy me."

Jamila showed Hamda how to tie one scarf on top of another, and she was right. It did look pretty.

"I like that," Hamda said. She chose five different scarves and began to tie them, first on one side, then the other, just like Jamila.

"I've done it!" she said as she tied the last one on top of her head. "I've done it! I'm wearing the veil, just like you!" And she ran to look in the mirror.

Oh dear.

Alya came to find her. "You haven't tried it my way," she said. "Wrap the scarf twice round your head, then tuck the end in by your cheek. See? Easy peasy!"

"I don't think it'll work," Hamda said sadly.

Hamda tried wrapping the scarf
twice round her head.

But she kept turning round and round,
and she got very dizzy.

The scarf slipped onto her shoulders.
"Oh no!" said Hamda.

She twisted the scarf to make it stay in place, but it tied itself round her waist instead of her head.

Hamda burst into tears. "I can't do it," she sobbed, and she went to find Mama.

Mama gave Hamda a hug. "Don't worry. Hind and Fatima and Jamila and Alya all found their own special way to wear the veil, and you will too. Now, come and help me find Dad's shoes. He's going out to the Mosque, and he can't find them anywhere."

Hamda was good at finding things.
In less than a minute she had found
Dad's shoes tucked underneath the
sofa. "Here they are!" she called.

"Thank you," said Dad, and he patted
her on the head. "My word! How big
you are growing! Soon you'll be as big
and beautiful as your sisters!"

Hamda didn't answer.
She was looking at Dad's shirt sleeves.
"What are those shiny things?"
she asked.

Dad held up his arm. "These are my cufflinks. My sleeves don't have any buttons, so I use these instead."

"So they hold the ends of your sleeves together?" Hamda said.

Dad laughed. "Exactly!"

"Oh." Hamda began to smile her special secret smile. She'd had an idea. She hugged Dad, and then she danced away.

"Hurrah! Hurrah!
I've found it!"

Dad scratched his head as he looked after her. "Hamda? What are you talking about?"

Hamda rushed up the stairs into her own room. She hunted through all her drawers, but she couldn't find what she was looking for.

Finally she looked in her toy basket and there, at the very bottom, was a pin. A shiny silver safety pin.

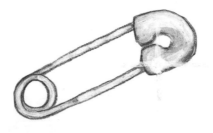

"Yes!" shouted Hamda.

She pulled on a hair cover and picked
up her beautiful black scarf with little
red roses.

Then, very very carefully, she pinned
the scarf under her chin.

"There!" she said. "That's what I wanted!"

Hamda did a twirl. The scarf stayed in place.

Hamda danced round the room. She jumped up and down.

She ran to look in Hind's big mirror.
The scarf was still there.
It hadn't moved at all.

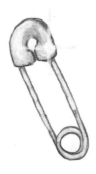

Five

Hamda rushed to the stairs.
Halfway down she checked.
The scarf was fine.

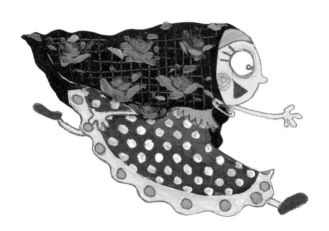

"Look!" Hamda said. "Look at me!
I'm wearing the veil! I'm a big girl!"
She did one twirl, and then another.
"Did you see?" she asked.

"I certainly did!" said Dad.
"Now I have five big daughters."

"You look **SO** grown up," said Mama.

Hind, Fatima, Jamila and Alya all began to clap. "Well done, Hamda!"

And Hamda smiled, but it wasn't
a secret smile. It was the biggest,
happiest smile ever.

She had found her own special way.